MAKING MONEY
– WITH –
SPORTS CARDS

THE ULTIMATE SIDE HUSTLE

NOAH BRISACH

MAKING MONEY WITH SPORTS CARDS

Copyright © 2020 by Noah Brisach

All rights reserved. No part of this publication may be reproduced, distributed, or transmitted in any form or by any means, including photocopying, recording, or other electronic or mechanical methods, without the prior written permission of the publisher, except in the case of brief quotations embodied in critical reviews and certain other noncommercial uses permitted by copyright law.

CONTENTS

CHAPTER 1   THE BREAKDOWN 1

CHAPTER 2   TYPES OF INVESTMENTS 6

CHAPTER 3   WHO TO BUY, WHEN TO BUY? 12

CHAPTER 4   GRADING & TRADING 20

CHAPTER 5   GETTING STARTED 26

CHAPTER 1

THE BREAKDOWN

It's not every day you can make a 150% return on your money because a hot young rookie you've been buying had a 30-point night. Or your team's number one prospect just got the call to the bigs. The best part about making money in this hobby is whether or not you have a $100 in the bank, or $100,000 in the bank, the following techniques can work for you. The sports card market is much like a roller-coaster ride. It takes, "what have you done for me lately", to new heights. Prices go up, and prices go down, like ticks on a stopwatch. You can use this as an advantage, or you can let it quickly diminish your bank account. It is important to know when, and why these prices fluctuate and to understand a good buy from a bad one. In the upcoming chapters, I will dive into the key components of the sports card market, and specific techniques that will help you establish and maintain a profitable side hustle, or even a full time career.

Just to give you an example of the profits that can be made in this hobby; A young Greek immigrant by the name of Giannis Antetokounmpo emerged into the basketball circuit as one of the games top players towards the end of his 2016/17 campaign. At this particular time, his PSA 10 Panini

Prizm rookie was sitting in the $100-range, give or take. That same card is currently selling on eBay for about $3500 currently, and has probably increased by the time you're reading this. That's a 35X profit, within a 3-year time span. No stock, real-estate, or bond investment on this planet will offer that kind of return. If you played your cards right, Giannis Antetokounmpo cards could've put your kids through college.

As a full disclosure, I want to let it be known that the techniques and insight I discuss throughout the course of this book are from my experience in the sports card market only. There are no guarantees in this business, or everyone would do it. I don't win on every deal I make, but you either win or you learn. Learn from each mistake and take note of it. Trial and error is the name of the game in this business. Once you find your niche, the profits will soon follow.

Hobby Breakdown

Baseball, football, and basketball are what keep this hobby running, in that exact order. However, that's not to say basketball can jump to the number one spot in this list, since it's the most rapidly growing sport worldwide. As popular as baseball and American football are, they're primarily followed in the United States, which limits the buyers in the market, and the potential for worldwide expansion. Football holds the largest price fluctuation, due to its relatively short season. All it takes is one horrible outing by a Quarterback, and with the snap of a finger, the profits you have been accumulating all offseason have gone to waste. On the other hand, if that same QB you invested in throws two deep balls and has a 400-yard win on opening day, you might be sitting on a pot of gold in your living room on a Sunday afternoon. I will further discuss the proper time frame that prices usually fall and rise, in chapter 3.

The Risk

Like I had previously mentioned, when money is involved, there is risk. Risk scares away plenty of novice investors when it comes to the ignorance of the market and uncertainty of price fluctuation. If you want to maintain profitability in this business, there are a few rules to follow. First and foremost, DO NOT BUY WHAT YOU CAN NOT AFFORD. It is important to maintain a proper budget that you spend on cards, and to not blow your whole paycheck on a Lebron rookie, when you have a mortgage, car payment, and a Netflix bill due next week. Pay your bills, then buy cards, so that eventually your profits from cards will take care of your bills. Buying boxes hoping you're going to pull the next Mike Trout will not help your profits either. Nine out of ten boxes will give you 20% of your money back if you are lucky. So was it really worth it? Ripping packs and giving people the gambling fix they think they need. The same sensation that a five-dollar scratch off brings, at a fraction of the price. If you have a gambling issue, you are fighting an uphill battle to be profitable in this hobby long term.

The Crowd

Following the crowd is setting yourself up for failure. If you followed the crowd last year and bought Baker Mayfield before the season started, thinking he was going to have an MVP type year, you might've gone bankrupt. This is a trap that many novices make as well. Their buddy introduces them to the hobby and how much money they made, so they blindly oblige to whatever players he tells him to buy without doing a single bit of research. In the long run, they both lose. You cannot be lazy and follow the crowd. Do your own research! This will pay dividends in the future, trust me. This is not to say a player that was recommended to you is always a bust, I'm just asking you to do your own research before you spend an absurd amount of money on a particular player. With that being said, there is no "perfect" window to buy or sell a particular player. That is up to you to determine after hours and hours of studying sold listings on eBay, trends of the player's prices, and the actual potential of the given player.

Hobby Appeal

Hobby appeal is the most important factor to understand today. It's tricky, and even the so-called experts have trouble determining it. What makes this player appealing to the market? This is a question you must ask yourself before any purchase. Is he in a large market team with a passionate fan base? Such as New York, or Los Angeles. Does he have the persona that makes people want to buy him? Plenty of guys in the hobby today have all the skills in the world, they just don't sell. Le'veon bell has been a top five running back just about every year he has been in the league. A three-time pro-bowler, two time first team all pro, and in the top five in all-purpose yards' year after year, but you can buy one of his autographs for $25 to $30, where an unproven rookie QB might be going for double or even triple that. I will break down each sport and the given factors that give players marketability and hobby appeal in the upcoming chapters.

Diversify

Before I get started, I'd like to touch on one last thing. Before you dive into the sports card investing world, it is important to lay out a plan, and write it down. Are you in this to make money within a few months? Or do you want your cards to gradually accumulate over years? I personally invest in both. I have certain guys that I believe have a ton of potential but might be stuck behind a good QB, or might have a few years left before they get the call to the majors, or a player who I believe will end up as an all-time great.

On the other hand, I like to keep money aside for flipping. This might entail buying football players during baseball season, then unloading come August or even a few weeks into the season. There is no "correct" way to invest. But as you get started on this journey, try to identify what works for you.

CHAPTER 2

TYPES OF INVESTMENTS

The sports card market has been trending in the right direction, and I believe it is only getting started. Once people start catching on that there can be more money made in a shorter time span than real-estate or the stock market, the sky's the limit. One of the greatest investors to ever walk the earth, Warren Buffet, earns an average of 20.5 percent return per year on his conglomerate Berkshire Hathaway. The same percentage return you can make buying a Lebron Rookie for $1000 in the offseason, waiting until he gets into the finals as he usually does, and unloading it then for $1200-$1250. Again, there is risk involved. However, Lebron either getting hurt, or his team not making the playoffs happened just once in the past fifteen years. I would label this as a low risk- low reward short term investment.

Short Term

A short term investment in the sports card world is anything within a twelve-month time span, from the time of purchas to the time of sell. As I prefer longer term investments, I understand that most people want to "get rich quick" and that time is of the essence. One of my favorite tried and true methods I had already mentioned, is buying in the off-season. Think the opposite of the crowd. If there is ever a guarantee in this madness, this might be it. The earlier in the off-season the better. The psychology of the market depicts the majority of the pricing in the market, therefore the off-season presents some of the best buying opportunities, simply because there is not much hype around that given sport at the time. A month or two after that given season has wrapped up, tend to offer the lowest prices. The wait time can be long and tedious, but will pay dividends if you unload at the right time. One example that has worked for me was buying Lamar Jackson cards in the early off-season of last year (2019) before his tremendous MVP campaign unfolded. He is a guy I was always high on since the draft, and knew it was only a matter of time before he made an impact in the NFL. However, I would not invest in him long term. He was strictly a short term investment for me and I knew that going in. With that being said, I am still high on him and believe he is a tremendous talent. However, I remain skeptical and question his play style long term. With being a primary running QB with designed run plays, his durability holding up throughout the upcoming years could be a risk factor for potential investors. I hate to make the comparison, but I'm going to do it anyway. Robert Griffin III possesses a similar playstyle to Jackson, and one bad injury changed the entire course of his career. He is now a third string QB, and soon might even be out of the league. There are many guys I run into at local card shows that hang their head in shame every time RG3's name is mentioned, knowing they invested a ton of money into a guy whose cards are now worthless. Again, I am a fan of Lamar Jackson, and I hope with my best intentions he dominates the league for years to come, and remains injury free while doing so.

FLIPPING CARDS

If you want to be serious about flipping you need to keep up to date with market prices and trends daily. This hobby is fickle, and prices literally change every day. Checking eBay sold listings is the most accurate way of determining the market. It is important to keep an excel doc of all the cards you are buying, and what you bought it for. A good template to start from is shown in the figure below.

Card	Date Purchased	Total Price Paid	Date Sold	Price Sold	Net Profit
2011 Mike Trout Topps Update PSA 10	4/22/19	($1,300)	5/27/19	1588	$288

This will give you a good foundation to keep track of your profits and losses, and will save you hours of grief trying to remember what you paid for a card. It can be tedious logging in every single purchase, but well worth it. Have a price target after every purchase that you would want to sell the item for, and write it down. Do the same for a limit you are willing to sell that card for, and cut your losses. The flipping game is not all sunshine and rainbows. You can lose money just as easy as you profit. For example, you buy a Prizm PSA 10 rookie of a guy you think might go deep into the playoffs. You purchase it right after the all-star break after it has already gone up a bit. You pay $150. A good risk/reward ratio to maintain profit is 2:1. You tell yourself you are willing to sell this card if it falls to $100, but you are willing to sell it if it climbs to $250. So you are risking $50 to make $100. You are not always going to hit this goal. Although, it is important to have a plan put in place before you invest your money.

Another flipping tactic that I've had success with in the past was to buy in bulk. Facebook card groups, and card forums seem to offer the best deals. EBay is difficult to profit on, but can be done. The taxes and fees eat into your profits. When buying lots, try to focus on no less than three cards, but no more than ten. Look for guys cards who are liquid. with hobby appeal that can be sold quickly and easily. The longer you sit on these cards, the longer their prices could plummet. When you are looking into buying a lot, do your research first. Check each individual card in that lot and check what they are selling for consistently on eBay. If you decide to resell on eBay. Subtract 13% of the average final sales. what you will be collecting per card.

For instance, say I am looking into buying a 6 card lot of Luka Doncic rookies for $600. Each one of them is selling for $120 on eBay. Sounds like easy money right? After you take out shipping and eBay fees, you are only pocketing about $104 on each card, which will give you a profit of about $24, that's if you can even sell each card for $120. So looking back, risking $600 to make $24 doesn't seem like the best investment. When buying lots, I would shoot for at least a 10% return on investment. This is of course after fees and taxes. Buying a lot on Facebook for $1000, with the intent to re-sell on eBay for $1300-1400 would be an example of a lot worthy of your time. After eBay takes their 13% of your $1350, you are still left with about $175 profit, which is a 17.5% return on your investment, and remember you bought it on Facebook, so you paid exactly $1000 and not a penny more.

Low-end Flips

This flipping technique is going to take plenty of time and effort, but can be very rewarding. The first step I would take in this process is to get yourself a roll of stamps, envelopes, a jumbo box of card savers, penny sleeves and a scale. You can get a roll of 100 stamps at your local post office to get you started for about .40 each. And the rest can be found on Amazon for relatively cheap. Once you have all the necessary materials, it's time to start buying. Your best bet is to search for a list of your local card shows or card shops. They are filled with $1, $2, and $3 boxes filled with hidden gems. This is where the hard work comes into play. Digging through these boxes at card shows is going to take you hours upon hours. Majority of these cards are thought of as "junk" by the dealer. So they create these boxes hoping they make enough off of them to pay for their table. But one man's trash, is another man's treasure. When you're digging through these boxes, keep in mind that you are looking to at least double your investment. With that being said, look for cards in $1 bins that you are confident you can sell for $2.50-$3 on eBay. Any card under $10, you can send in the mail using a plain white envelope(PWE), as long as you let the buyer know in your description. This can save you $3-4 per card, and will allow you to charge "free shipping" which is appealing to buyers. This is where the scale comes in. As long as your envelope is under 1 oz., you should be able to get away with only one stamp. You need to look at the bigger picture when using this method. Selling 25 of these low-end cards per week might only net you $50-$75, but an extra $50 a week is an extra $2600 per year.

LONG TERM

This method of investing seems to be the least appealing, but holds some of the best opportunities. If you are still seeking to "get rich quick", this method isn't for you. Long term investing allows you to accumulate wealth over a period of years. Having to put cards in your safe box and keep them under your bed for several years collecting dust is something you have to get used to. I like to only use this method when looking long term in a player's career. Guys who need time for development, or guys that you think will end up in the hall of fame. Stephen Curry is a prime example. He didn't light the world on fire his first few years in the league. This gave long term investors a great opportunity to buy. Those couple of years of letting Curry's cards collect dust paid off. I'm sure some couldn't wait any longer and sold prematurely, but patience is a virtue with this method. If the strong believers held until he won back to back MVP awards, they cashed in on quite the payday.

CHAPTER 3

WHO TO BUY, WHEN TO BUY?

As I touched on before, there is no correct answer to this question. However, I am here to point you in the right direction. Each sport generally has specific timeframes throughout a given year when their prices become more affordable. Usually, there is a reason for this. The main reason lies as a result of impatience of most investors. The idea of holding cards more than a year baffles people, in which it definitely shouldn't. It is important to hang tough when a card dips for a few months because the season is so far away. If you have given up on that particular player and think he has no chance at turning it around like you had hoped, then maybe it is time to cut your losses and move on. Although, if you truly believe in a guy, you shouldn't fall into this trap and hold like you had planned.

The best way to explain this pattern is to buy what everyone else isn't. So in July and August when football fever is heating up, and baseball is in full swing, guess what you should buy. Basketball! If you don't know about basketball, do yourself a favor, and learn. Basketball is the fastest growing sport in this hobby, and has a unique opportunity to grow worldwide. A novelty that football and baseball do not have at this given moment. I know this method doesn't make for the best stories to tell your buddies, and you sure as hell won't make a 10x profit over night because so and so dropped fifty on the Lakers, but as I mentioned, it provides good buying windows for future investments. As far as who to buy. There are definitely guys who have more hobby appeal then others, and sell a lot easier.

BASEBALL

When buying baseball there are a few products that I would put above the rest. Starting with Bowman. The first Bowman of any given player is generally their most coveted card, and rightfully so. It's their very first card in their pro uniform. When looking to invest in any prospects, I would start with the 1st Bowman Chrome autographs. They are on-card autographs, which usually adds value in collector's eyes, they usually put out a very sleek design, and they are generally affordable, unless there is a hype train a thousand miles long on the guy. 1st Bowman's have a series of refractor cards that have serial numbers given by Topps, giving the population of that specific card. They are in the form of colored parallel cards. The base refractor numbered to 499, then comes the purple /250, blue, /150, gold /50, orange /25, red /5, and the holy grail of all first Bowman's. The superfractor numbered to only one.

Prospect investing is not for the faint of heart. The profits can be big if you do your research and your guy ends up panning out, but your losses can be huge. Think of it this way, about 66% of guys drafted in the first round get the call up to the bigs, which means 34% of guys don't even play in the major leagues in every draft! The draft in the MLB is like no other sport. Usually, in football or basketball, the first rounder's have the opportunity to play that exact year. Baseball players usually have a series of years getting paid minimum wage in some middle of nowhere farm team just before they can make an impact on the franchise that had drafted them. For this reason alone, you should understand the risk that goes into prospecting. In my eyes, it's a high risk/high reward way of investing. However, there is a general misconception that I would like to point out when investing in prospects. Usually, investors do not like using this method because they believe they'll have to wait three or four years before their guy gets called up to the majors, before they can unload the cards they bought. This is not the case. Prospects go up in price for a multitude of reasons. They might have a three home run night, or a 10 game hit streak, or even getting promoted from AA to AAA will cause a huge spike in price. The technique that I used pretty effectively and still use to this day is buying AAA guys that should get the call to the big leagues that year. December and January gives you the best entry point for these guys, right before the spring training buying spree begins.

Topps flagship is another product I would recommend. This is the regular Topps brand release every year before the season, and Topps Update is released after the all-star break, including any rookies that got called up that given year. You can usually get it at Target or Walmart. If you ever have to each to open packs for relatively low cost, Topps Series 1 and 2 are generally fun breaks. They have a series of short printed photo variations to hunt for and plenty of packs to open up for the money.

Perhaps the most important question when investing in baseball. What type of players should I focus on? Very simply put, home run hitters! There is no way around this. Dingers sell. Dj Lemahieu leads the league in average every other year and you can't give his cards away. Tim Anderson of the Chicago White Sox hit .335 last years and his 1st Bowman Auto sells for $20-$25. Why do you think that is? He only hit 18 bombs. The list goes on and on, but all the guys that sell with the exception of very few, hit home runs, and a lot of them. Guys like Mike Trout, Aaron Judge, Cody Bellinger, Mookie Betts.

I know what you're thinking. What about pitchers? As far as I'm concerned, they're in the same boat as contact hitters, maybe even worse. Arguably the best pitcher to sling it in the modern era, Clayton Kershaw is relatively inexpensive, and has never experienced a significant price increase, despite all of his successes, in the regular season that is. He's a Dodger. One of the most passionate fan bases in all of sports. He's a three-time Cy Young Winner. One of those seasons he was awarded NL MVP. But he still never reached the prices of the top tier hitters of his era like Trout, Pujols, and even Miggy.

The dreaded name in every pitcher's nightmares. Tommy John. For some, it's inevitable, for investors, it's dreadful. Tommy John surgery takes a full year away from players at the minimum. After surgery, recovery, and rehab is complete, they could have missed two full years. That's two years your cards aren't appreciating. I stay away from pitchers for this reason alone. The risk is not worth the reward.

FOOTBALL

Products I would start focusing on when it comes to football Prizm, Optic, National Treasures, and Contenders. The holy grail of all football rookie cards is the Contenders rookie ticket, similar to baseballs 1st bowman card. Tom Brady's rookie ticket auto dabbles into the half million-dollar range. When it was released in 2000, you would have been lucky to sell it for $100. However, collectors and investors seem to be catching on to the appeal Contenders and National Treasures brings, driving the prices of these products to the moon. This year's NT is selling for $1100 a pack, and continuing to rise. The likelihood of pulling a top tier QB that would exceed that $1100 price point is extremely low. But hey, if you really can't resist the temptation, be my guest. You might get lucky and pull a Kyler Murray RPA worth five grand. The bread and butter of the football rookie hobby is the Prizm rookies. They are coveted, and decently priced. Any time I am looking to invest in a guy that's the first thing I buy. They offer colored variations as far as the eyes can see. However, I've had plenty of success with flipping the base rookies. I've been buying Drew Lock and Kyler Murray base prizms since the product released, anywhere from $5-$10. Lock then sold in August for $40 per and Murray is up around $50 per, and that with neither of them playing a single snap in the offseason. Where else could you 10X your money in a matter of months? Patrick Mahomes is a guy I always regret not investing in. It haunts me to this day that I passed up on his base Prizms time and time again while they were $5 a piece, give or take. It kills me to say that the same card now sells regularly for $7000 in a psa 10. Yes, you read that correct. What If I bought a couple hundred of those at $5 each, instead of spending hundreds on Mitchell Trubisky who, in my opinion, should be making his way to a backup role very shortly. Hindsight is always 20/20 of course, but it's tough to forget such a missed opportunity.

What type of players should you buy in football? If you're serious about making money in this hobby, there's really only one answer to this question, and its Quarterbacks. They're really the only position worth investing in. Of course this is my opinion, however, it's tough to name one running back, receiver, or defensive guy that has appreciated and maintained their value from their rookie year on. Adrian Peterson took the hobby by storm in 2007. Arguably had the most hype around him of any college player in the past decade. His cards are far from worthless today, but I would say they are about half the price they were back then. Here's a guy who had just about as good of a career as any RB. Rookie of the year, eclipsed 2000 rushing yards in a single season, comeback player of the year after an apparent, "career ending" injury. Then of course the infamous MVP year. He seemed to accomplish nearly anything a running back could ever desire. Aside from a super bowl ring. Next time you think an upcoming rookie back is a "good buy", think back to AP. As far as wide receivers go, they aren't far behind backs. High risk, low reward. I can't quite pinpoint exactly why the hobby appeal is so low for receivers. However, Larry Fitzgerald is a guy that beat the odds, and ended up being a great investment since his rookie year and will be heading to Canton when its all said and done. His cards seem to appreciate in value nearly every year. Finding guys like this is like finding a needle in a haystack. I think wide outs do offer better buying opportunities than running backs, but not nearly the opportunity Qb's present.

When looking to buy quarterbacks, keep in mind that there's only going to be one or two that pan out each draft class. One of the best Qb classes of all time was 2004, and just three panned out. Eli Manning, Ben Roethlesberger, and Phillip Rivers. Each year, there are going to be some guys that are at a very appealing price point. Usually there is a reason. Maybe that team already has their starting QB, and they drafted him for a backup role only. Maybe they drafted him to learn the offense and groom him to be the starter years from now. Whatever the case may be, it's important to know what makes a QB a "good buy". Of course the hobby appeal is always the leading factor in the drive of prices, however, pay attention to the hype. Look at what teams are building up their offense and defense. Maybe signing a big wide out or running back, all still in search for their guy under center. It only takes a year for a team to do a complete 180. The Niners went from the laughing stock of the league, to a super bowl contender all within a year or two. Look what teams have an aging or injury prone QB, likely on his way out. All it takes is an ESPN update of a team promoting that teams current backup to the starting position, and prices could double.

BASKETBALL

There may have never been a better time to invest in basketball cards than right now. The appeal is there just as much as any other sport. As I discussed earlier in the book, the basketball hobby has the best opportunity for growth. Simply put, it's the only world renown sport of the three. Especially with guys like Giannis and Luka Doncic coming from overseas, the talent pool in the NBA is growing with intriguing young talent. The rise of Zion Williamson helped send the hobby into the stratosphere. Once the highly coveted Panini Prizm dropped, investors flooded Targets and Walmarts like a pack of wolves, buying out entire inventories. Although I believe Zion is a phenomenal talent and his cards will appreciate in value over time, but I do not however he is the "next Lebron". His prices are at the point right now where he is almost projected to be better than LeBron. All the hype behind him is a result of people comparing his game to others. In reality, do you really think this kid is going to surpass Lebron James? If so, you should stop reading right now and buy as many Zions you can afford. Once again, some of the best buying opportunities are the guys who people aren't buying. For example, Coby White and Ja Morant. With a sensational first half of his rookie season, Ja put up exceptional numbers for a rookie, causing his prices to rise. All it took was a minor injury from Zion for investors to switch gears and buy Ja. His base prizms went from $10 to $50 rather quickly. Coby White on the other hand, had himself three straight games with 30 points. The price of his prizm Silver tripled overnight. I am not saying to stay away from guys like Zion, but think to yourself, does this guy's prices really have room to grow? As far as which products to focus on when buying basketball, focus on the big three. Panini Prizm, Select, and Donruss Optic. These products continue to gain popularity for many reasons. As noted in Football, the Prizm rookie is the most highly regarded rookie card of any given player. Much like the Contenders rookie ticket in football, the Prizm silver is the holy grail of basketball rookies. Giannis' PSA 10 prizm silver is in the $15k range currently, and I am almost positive it will increase by the time you read this as well. There is not really a certain position to buy in basketball, however, there are positions to stay away from in general. Centers and Power forwards do not sell as well as the other three positions do, however there are exceptions. Anthony Davis is a guy whose prices have been ascending his entire career. Of course Shaq, has maintained his value very well.

There are a few traps that card investors fall into year after year. Buying the name. How many of your favorite college players ended up panning out in the League? Guys like Jimmer Fredette, Doug Mcdermott, Hasheem Thabeet, Darko Milicic. Part of the game is seeking for guys that will adjust well at the next level. Some players just cannot make the adjustment. Of course, none of us are professional NBA scouts, but doing your research properly can help you point these guys out.

CHAPTER 4

GRADING & TRADING

In my opinion, the most lucrative process in all of sports cards is grading, if done correctly. There are plenty of investors that make a living off of buying cards, grading them, and collecting the profits. The profit margins are always there. Even in "bad submissions" you should usually at least make your money back. There are a few tips I can share with you that will save you time and money in the long run. Patience is inevitable when it comes to grading. If you're willing to wait a little bit, your patience will pay off, if not, grading is not for you.

First and foremost, there are a few supplies you will want to purchase before you start submitting your cards to grade. You are going to need card savers. I recommend you buy them in bulk. If you are not familiar with card savers, they are the preferred holders in grading submissions by both Beckett and PSA. They make it extremely easy to maneuver in and out of the holder, preventing any further damage to the card during the grading process. You can purchase this on eBay for relatively cheap. Next come the cleaning materials. A good microfiber cloth is needed to wipe your cards down before submitting. Do not wipe your cards with anything else. You'd be surprised how easy cards can scratch. A jewelry magnifier is always a plus but not needed. This will allow you to get a closer look at the corners of your cards. Meguirs Scratch X 2.0 is what I use to clean surfaces that need more than just a wipe down with a microfiber.

PSA and Beckett are the two most popular grading companies and the only two I have ever used. Although you will pay the highest rates with these two companies, their "9.5" or "10" label holds more credibility to most collectors, which is why cards in their slab sell the highest. With that being said, they both follow the same criteria when grading cards. They grade corners, surface, centering, and edges. When looking for potential candidates to grade, always remember these criteria. Each submission, you will get a better feel for what cards will gem and what will not. Keep in mind, it is very possible to fix surface issues, and even some corners. If the centering or edges have issues, the card likely will not gem. Another variable when determining good cards to submit to grade, are price comparisons. Look at what the card is selling for ungraded, and compare it to the price of that card in a GEM. If there's only a slight difference in price, it's not a good card to grade. As crazy as this sounds, a good way of telling if it's a good grading candidate is to double the raw price of the card, and If that price less than what the gem price is, it's a good candidate. For example, a Trae Young Prizm rookie is selling for about $50. This exact card is selling consistently for $200+ in a GEM. That is a 4x profit opportunity, and definitely worth a grading submission.

It's important to understand where to buy cards worthy of a gem. Unfortunately, most sellers on eBay are the furthest thing from honest, when explaining the condition of their cards. If the card is in such impeccable shape, why don't they just grade it themselves? The quick question is, because there's usually something wrong with it. However, I have had success in the past buying cards on eBay that eventually came back as gems. It is fairly easy determining the centering and corners from the picture or scan they provide. However, the surface and edges are nearly impossible to determine. What I like to do is focus my buying on guys with high feedback ratings of 100%. Then I simply send them a quick message saying, "are there any surface or edge flaws?" If they do not respond, on to the next card. If they do, they will generally tell you the truth since they have a good feedback rating. This is not always the case, but I give them more credit than a dude with horrible feedback. I have had the most success purchasing "future gems" at card shows. Most dealers allow you to look at the card up close, and some even let you take it out of the holder. The more grading you do, you will be able to spot a gem within ten seconds of looking at it up close.

Another tip I would like to give you, is to focus on cards that you believe will appreciate in value while they are getting graded. For example, send in a football order in April or May. As the season approaches, your cards should go up anyway. If they come back gems, that's icing on the cake. If they come back with lower grades than you expected, you might still be able to break even. Like I said, it should be difficult to come out on the losing end of a grading submission as it is, that is if you are patient. PSA and Beckett can take months on end, so get ready to wait. Start by sending in small submissions. Five to ten cards that you are very confident in getting good grades. What I like to do is predict what grade my cards will receive. Be completely honest with yourself. This will give you a good gauge on your expectations vs PSA or Beckett. Your first couple submissions might not be exactly what you expected. But each and every submission, your confidence will grow. Then your five card orders will turn to twenty card orders, then fifty, etc.

Group submissions is the best way to go in terms of pricing. Guys who run group submissions get offered lower rates because the quantity in which they send. Instead of going right through the grading company paying $25-$30 a card. Most group subs offer a much cheaper rate. You can find these guys on Facebook groups mostly, and some of them have their own Instagram accounts. Most of them have a good reputation and are easy to work with. If you ever have any questions on how the process works, send them a quick message, and they should get back to you fairly easily. If you really don't mind the wait, bulk submissions are the way to go. The turnaround times on these submissions are much longer, but the rates are significantly cheaper.

Once PSA and Beckett grade their cards, they will put them in protective cases with the final grade written on it. The last thing I will touch on in regards to grading is the idea of cracking these cases and re-subbing. It is important to know the risk involved when attempting this. In layman's terms, the idea is to crack open an already graded card case, whether it be PSA or Beckett, cleaning it, then resubmitting the card in hopes of getting a higher grade. As you might already know, the difference in a PSA 9 and a PSA 10, could be hundreds, or even thousands of dollars. What I would recommend before you go cracking five figure cards, is to buy some low end Beckett and low end PSA cards, and practice cracking those. I learned as easy as watching a YouTube video, and cracking some old PSA and Beckett slabs I had laying around. With a little practice, it can be a very simple process. When I do this, I usually shoot for Beckett slabs that only need a .5 bump in one of the subgrades to bump the full grade of the card up. For example, a good cracking candidate would be a card with 9.5 centering, 9.5 edges, 9 corners, and 9 surface. This way all you need is a .5 increase on corners or surface to bump the card to a Gem (9.5). To show you the price differential on just a minor .5 bump, A Mike Trout 2011 Bowman Chrome rookie card consistently sells for $450-$650 in a BGS 9. The BGS 9.5 goes for about $900-$1200.Cracking and re-subbing doesn't even cross the mind of an average investor due to the risk factor, but with a little practice and perseverance, you could add it to your arsenal of investing techniques to put you above the rest.

TRADING

I don't usually trade as often as I used to, but there are plenty of ways for you to use trading to your advantage. First and foremost, it is very important that you keep track of what you paid for every card you own. If you don't know exact pricing, then give it a ballpark estimate. Without knowing prices, you have into cards, make it very easy to get the short end of the stick in while making a trade, especially in person. When trading in person, whether it be at a card show or your local card shop, you have less time to make decisions and could easily get ripped. Whether or not you can determine the price you have put into a specific card, it is a good idea to establish a fair "trade value". This however, is not always the same as the sale price of that card. It could be a bit higher or lower depending on how you value the card. What I usually do is look at recent eBay sales, usually within a week or two, then I value my card accordingly. If I am really high on a guy, I might set a higher trade value, or only accept specific cards in exchange for my card.

"Trading up" and "trading down" are two strategies I would recommend focusing on while trading. Trading up is basically trading multiple cards for one high end card. For example, trading five $50 rookies in exchange for one $250 card. This is good for collectors who are looking to focus more on quality than quantity. Trading down is just the opposite. Trading a $250 card for five $50 cards.

Another method that worked for me in the past was trading guys who I believed would depreciate in value, for guys I thought would appreciate. This seems fairly obvious, but it's a great way at getting in on an investment when you don't have the funds to. For example, trading a guy that you believe is at his peak price; whether it be a guy who just won a ring, or a hot prospect that you might not be that high on, for guys that might be undervalued, or currently in the off-season. When trading online, make sure you set a specific day that you and the member you made the trade with both send your items out. This makes it very simple for both parties, and avoids any confusion and possible scamming. If you really aren't comfortable with trading yet, try convincing the guy to send first, and provide you a tracking number. Then you can send your package out after you receive it.

CHAPTER 5

GETTING STARTED

I've been attending card shows as far as I can remember. My dad has always been into the hobby since he was a kid. He introduced me to it by letting me tag along to shows with him. I stayed out of my mom's hair and got to learn some business all at once. It wasn't until high school until I really started getting into the money making side of the hobby. Long story short, I pulled a Mike Trout autograph out of a single Topps Finest pack, sold it for a few thousand during my gym class the next day, and never looked back. Currently, I don't really collect anyone. There are a couple reasons for this. The main reason is that I started so many collections that I missed out on a ton of opportunities to make money. It's difficult to make money when you're collecting all the guys everyone wants. I'd be lying if I said I miss collecting, but I truly enjoy the process of sports card investing. That itself is a passion of mine. It has given me the knowledge of the foundations of entrepreneurship, before I knew what that word even meant. If I were to give advice to someone that wants to enjoy both sides of the hobby, both collecting and investing, it would be to focus on one specific player. Start a personal collection of one guy, and one guy only that you really enjoy collecting. This will keep your mind sane and allow you to enjoy this hobby a little more, while making some money at the same time.

With that being said, anyone can be introduced to this hobby at any point in life. Sure it helps to have a father with all the knowledge of the hobby already, but I truly believe anyone can turn this hobby to their own personal side hustle. It is going to take plenty of hours of price research, market trends and attending card shows. Usually there is an online schedule of card shows in your area. Most local malls and convention centers hold them at least a few times annually. Facebook groups are great starting points to get a grasp of market movers and popular trends in the hobby. Don't ever be afraid of asking questions if you're ever unsure about something. Nobody knows everything, and most guys will be happy to answer your questions and see a new guy in the hobby.

When it comes to attending card shows, it is very easy to become overwhelmed. Making a list of guys you are looking for is never a bad idea. Keep the list short however. I usually go with one guy from each sport in mind that I am "looking for", but I always keep my options open. Often I end up leaving the show with cards of guys that I never had planned on buying. With the proper knowledge of the market, I could determine what is a good deal or what is not in an instant. Card shows are where price knowledge can really pay off. If you did your homework, shows will usually provide the best deals. Just a few months ago I approached a table that had a Ronald Acuna rookie card that I had wanted, priced at $475. The show I usually attend is in the basement of a casino, so I was unable to look up the recent sale price of the card, with no internet connection on my phone. Therefore, I went to the parking lot, to see the card was consistently selling on eBay for $600+. I rushed back into the show like a mad man and went back to buy it. It sold that quickly. I was devastated. Me not knowing the price of that card cost me a potential $125 profit. Patience is a virtue at card shows. Oftentimes I find myself looking to find deals right away. Sometimes you do, most times you won't. Depending on how big the show is, I like to see every table at least once before I buy. Unless there is a deal that just can't be passed up on, it pays to look around. Most tables have roughly the same cards which can help drive down the prices.

It's also important to establish a budget before you attend a show. It can be very easy to spend much more than you intended to. Take as much cash as you plan to spend. ATM's will eat your money up at most venues. Also, ask yourself what kind of cards you're looking to buy. Are you looking for strictly high end cards in the display cases? Or are you trying to find hidden gems in the bargain bins. I usually allocate a day for each. This gives me plenty of time for both while avoiding the stress of being short on time. Some guys can spend full weekends at shows fishing through bargain bins, and make out very well. As far as what to bring to the show. First and foremost, bring a backpack. I don't care how old you are; you will thank me later. In that backpack, you should bring whatever cards you'd like to either sell or trade to the dealers. Also, bring some holders and penny sleeves. Some dealers don't always have proper holders to project your cards as they rattle around in your backpack. With that being said, make sure the backpack has pockets to keep your cards secure. Backpacks are also good to throw your coat in during winter shows, so you have two hands when fishing through boxes. Most of the bigger shows invite grading and authentication companies, so keep that in mind while you pack your backpack. Each avenue of buying and selling has its share of pros and cons. However, there are a few I would recommend starting out with. EBay is where I do the majority of my dealing. It's probably the most accurate site to determine accurate market trends, and it reaches the largest audience.

With that being said, you are paying for these services. EBay will take 10% of your final sales plus another approximate 3% on top due to PayPal fees. So roughly thirteen percent of your sale price is gone before you collect your money. It's important to factor these fees when determining your profit. There are eBay fee calculators all over the web to help determine how much will end up getting taken out. On the other hand, purchases you make on eBay will also be taxed. This tax varies depending on the state, but you'll generally be looking at another 5%-10% on top of the price you win it for.

There's a few ways to avoid paying these fees. I've mentioned Facebook groups quite a few times throughout the course of the book for good reason. I feel as if most investors are simply getting tired with eBay's shenanigans, and are looking elsewhere. When you're looking to get into a Facebook group, look at the number of members the group has first. I usually look for 5000 members before I request to join. This shows that the group has a dedicated admin team and are dedicated to their groups success. There are even certain groups allocated to certain products. For example, I am in a couple of Panini Prizm only groups that I like to buy and sell on. Facebook groups allow you to interact with guys on a personal level and even develop friendships with. I've dealt with a couple guys so many times they come to me first before they post their cards to the public. If you ever doubt the security of these groups, there are even groups that you can join that specifically focus on exposing scammers in the Facebook card community. Facebook allows you to deal straight through PayPal. Therefore, the 10% eBay fee is then avoided, and your payment is still insured. In case anything went wrong, you file a dispute with PayPal and they should refund you your money. The problem with this is, other guys will try talking you down simply by saying, "C'mon you're saving the eBay fees", meanwhile, they're avoiding eBay fees as well, in which they conveniently forget to mention. If people like this refuse to budge, simply move onto the next customer. Another negative aspect of these groups are the audience size. You are only reaching out to a few thousand people, where on eBay you are reaching the entire world. However, the number of members in these groups are growing each and every day. I could see myself dealing full time on Facebook in the near future.

With the purchase of this book, I am granting you my personal email address to ask me anything you desire about learning the market and I will be happy to answer. Please email me with any questions that you are left unanswered after reading this at noahbrisach3@gmail.com. With this hobby so rapidly evolving, the opportunities for you as an investor are endless. Don't let anyone talk you out of it, and it's never too late to start. God bless your journey and never give up!

www.ingramcontent.com/pod-product-compliance
Lightning Source LLC
Chambersburg PA
CBHW050324220526
45465CB00005B/2121